MARTHA'S VINEYARD
IN COLOR

MARTHA'S VINEYARD
in Color

A Collection of Color

Photographs by

JULIUS LAZARUS

With Text and

Notes on the Illustrations by

MARION VUILLEUMIER

HASTINGS HOUSE · PUBLISHERS

New York, 10016

PUBLISHED 1979 BY HASTINGS HOUSE, PUBLISHERS, INC.

Library of Congress Cataloging in Publication Data
Lazarus, Julius.
    Martha's Vineyard in color.

    (Profiles of America)
    1. Martha's Vineyard, Mass.—Description and travel. I. Vuilleumier, Marion.
II. Title. F72.M5L39   1979   917.44'94'0440222   79-4299
ISBN 0-8038-4724-6

Published simultaneously in Canada by
Saunders, of Toronto, Ltd., Don Mills, Ontario

Printed and bound in Hong Kong by Mandarin Publishers Limited

*Dedicated to Eva R. and
Lori B. Lazarus*

ACKNOWLEDGEMENTS

*Appreciation is expressed to the many people
who provided information, especially Vineyarders
Peg and William Littlefield, Beatrice Vanderhoop Gentry,
Bertha Vanderhoop Giles, Jon and Ann Nelson,
as well as former summer Vineyarders
Philip and Anita Buddington along with
Marian Logan who typed the manuscript.*

CONTENTS

An Undefeated Insularity

I

THERE IS SOMETHING MAGICAL about an island, even one tucked so closely to the skirts of Massachusetts as Martha's Vineyard. This refuge from chaotic America is only seven miles off Cape Cod, yet to those who know and love it it's another world altogether. For those who discover it for the first time it's an amazing serendipity experience. Where else can one stand on a windswept beach in sight of the mainland and inhale air as fresh and pure as if it were thirty miles out to sea? Where else can one instinctively sense as soon as one's foot touches a flat, outwash landing field or a weather-beaten deck edged by the sea that this triangular-shaped glacial remnant is a very special place?

The island's sage, Henry Beetle Hough—from his vantage point of more than five decades, most of these as editor of the *Vineyard Gazette*—says Martha's Vineyard's magic lies in its contradictions. In his book *Martha's Vineyard* (beautifully illustrated by the noted photographer Alfred Eisenstadt) Hough writes, "Civilization has changed, progressed, moved on, adopted new patterns of convenience, settled into habits of its own age; and Martha's Vineyard is involved as all other places in this age and this civilization; yet it retains its flavor, purposes, character. Its basic challenges and decisions rest in the balance between man and nature, sea and shore . . . Modern yet not modern, ancient but not ancient, the island's contradictions are themselves an elusive but genuine expression of an undefeated insularity."

Isolation is of course part of the magic of any island. To the visitor, isolation heightens the interest because it is so utterly opposite to the life at home. Don't they say opposites attract? Isolation breeds a strong individualism, initiative, and self-reliance on the part of the inhabitants of an island. On the Vineyard, for example, the telephone company had begun as a local enterprise founded by a doctor. Ma Bell at the time saw no profit in stringing phone lines along thinly populated country lanes on islands. But Dr. Charles F. Lane's patients lived down those country lanes and needed phones, so he built a line and founded a company which was later taken over by the Bell Telephone Company. The electric light company had also begun as a local enterprise, established by a former steamboat captain.

This same isolation affects all life on the island—not just humans. Some species shaped by isolation become slightly different from their former selves. Even if they remain the same they are given provincial names. The high pitched tinkling of the spring peepers (Hyla Crucifer) are a reminder that peep frogs are known on Martha's Vineyard, and nowhere else, as pinkletinks.

Beyond the contradictions and the isolation there is a variety of activity which adds to the magic of this island. As Harvey Ewing, Bureau Chief of the *Cape Cod Times,* wrote recently, "A microcosm of New England in summer can be found on Martha's Vineyard . . . a piece of land in the Atlantic Ocean measuring 67,700 acres and designed by Nature and man to provide the type of vacation to satisfy a variety of tastes." The Vineyard offers all that can be enjoyed at any seashore, he notes, along with the pastoral beauty of an English countryside. Windswept moors and marshes can be seen along with even more ancient geological formations like the breathtakingly rainbow-hued clay cliffs at Gay Head. For those who prefer woods and lakes there is a state forest along with innumerable interior ponds and many wildlife sanctuaries. The sports minded can whack golf balls, mount riding horses, or seek out a profusion of other sports and games. History buffs take the house tours and tread reverently through museums. In addition, there are shops, shops, and more shops!

Another aspect of this island's magic is its capsule view of living history. There are very few places on this continent where, captured in such a few miles, are evidences of the earliest inhabitants as well as those of today, with all stages in between represented. The Wampanoags, descendants of Martha's Vineyard's earliest residents, are still here, exceedingly proud of their ancient heritage, especially in Gay Head where Vanderhoops, Smalleys, Jeffers, Mannings and Madisons carry on their traditions.

Descendants of the early English settlers are here too. On mailboxes are lettered Allen, Cottle, Daggett, Luce, Norton, Pease, and Mayhew. There are currently 19 Mayhews listed in the telephone book, descendants of Thomas Mayhew, who in 1641 purchased the Vineyard, along with Nantucket and the Elizabeth Islands, from the Earl of Stirling. A walk by the mansions of whaling captains on North Street in Edgartown is a reminder that "by 1825 the name of

Edgartown was known around the globe as a whaling port and birthplace of doughty mariners" according to Eleanor Ransome Mayhew, writing in *Martha's Vineyard, A Short History and Guide.* That era ended in 1838 when two chemists in a shed in Waltham, Massachusetts, refined kerosene from petroleum and the bottom fell out of the whalers' market.

Then came the day of resorts. A stroll through the Hansel-and-Gretel-like Camp Meeting grounds at Oak Bluffs reveals that some vacationers came for religious reasons, while a visit to the famous Flying Horses, America's oldest carousel on nearby Circuit Avenue, is evidence of more secular drawing cards. A thicket of sails in the harbor is a reminder that the squadron of the New York Yacht Club has visited annually since well before the turn of the century.

Recent days have made this a celebrity haven. Whether it is television newsman Walter Cronkite in his 43-foot yacht *Wyntje,* or the movie *Jaws* being filmed, day-trippers and vacationers in midsummer can usually return home bragging about the luminaries they have bagged with their cameras. Both of these incidents represent history that will be looked back on with awe some future day.

Have you been tantalized enough? If you haven't already succumbed to the island's charm, are you ready to listen to its siren song? Come. Cast off with me.

II

THERE ARE MANY WAYS to reach Martha's Vineyard. Planes fly in regularly from east coast cities and from the Barnstable airport in Hyannis. Boats steam faithfully over the water from harbors in New Bedford, Woods Hole, Hyannis, as well as Falmouth inner harbor. Private vessels and charter boats sail into its welcoming harbors. My favorite pathway to the Vineyard begins at the ferry slip in Woods Hole, where the Steamship Authority proudly boasts it has been "lifeline to the islands since 1818."

We arrive early, clattering up the companionways to locate our deck chairs in the choicest viewing spot. Leaning over the railing we see across the murky emerald expanse, the ponderous, top-heavy Alcoa *Sea Probe,* patiently awaiting at her berth the next expedition to discover more secrets of the sea. Below there is a constant rattle of the gang plank as cars, busses, and trucks stream through the ferry's open mouth into its cavernous maw. The harbor bustles and hums around us continuously almost unnoticed while we watch two Coast Guard helicopters hover solicitously over channel buoys. Then we stare in disbelief as six beautiful horses ride serenely by on a high-fenced barge. They are being towed by a small cruiser to Naushon Island, we are told, that exclusive territory of the Boston

Forbeses. It seems horses furnish the only transportation on that island except for one more highly horsepowered truck.

Our reverie about long-ago ways on a today island is abruptly broken by the ferry's penetrating bellow, announcing that it is about to sail. Soon we are in mid-channel and the island on the horizon is rapidly becoming larger. During the 45-minute trip we watch the sun lay a platinum path on the water and illumine the alabaster wings of hovering gulls.

As we enter Vineyard Haven harbor, which is at the apex of the triangular shaped island, we sail between two projecting arms which seem to welcome us. Each point of land—East Chop and West Chop—has its lighthouse standing as a silent sentinel. With engines rumbling the ferry docks fussily and begins to disgorge its contents. We descend into the dockside confusion of the community originally called Holmes Hole. Welcoming relatives throw their arms around newcomers. Jitney drivers hopefully call "Taxi to all points" and "Anywhere on the island." We pick our way through the crowd to the car rental booth and a waiting Aspen.

Lots of unhurried time is needed to appreciate this island, but today's trip is a survey of many of its out-standing points and a car is the best helper. Whether you spend a month, a year, or a day, or whether you travel by foot, bicycle, or motor, a good guide book is essential. We like *Exploring Martha's Vineyard,* written by summer resident Polly Burroughs and pleasingly illustrated by Robert James Pailthorp's sketches and maps.

"Before you go anywhere on Martha's Vineyard", says the author, "you should know what the Vineyarders mean by 'down-Island' and 'up-Island.' These terms originated many years ago with seamen who, as they sailed in an easterly direction, decreased or ran 'down' their degree of longitude toward zero at Greenwich, England. A westbound ship was, in turn, running 'up' its longitude. Thus 'down-Island' refers to the easterly side of the Island, including Vineyard Haven, Oak Bluffs, Edgartown, and Chappaquiddick. 'Up-Island' is the western portion, including North and West Tisbury, Chilmark, and Gay Head. The 4,300-acre Martha's Vineyard State Forest and airport are considered 'mid-Island'."

We take off down-Island direction to the tiny summer colony of Oak Bluffs. (We shall come back to visit Vineyard Haven—the ferry docking point—later.) A drive along the shore brings us to Ocean Park, a semi-circular green fringed by charming, gingerbread-trimmed, wooden houses which overlook the ocean. Set like a jewel in the velvety lawn is a white, octagonal bandstand, the scene of concerts on summer evenings, but now just a lace-like decoration.

Just back of this somnolent scene is a bustling harbor and Circuit Avenue with its welter of shops, galleries, and antique stores. Here too is what the National Carousel Roundtable declares is the oldest carousel in the nation. Dating to the 1870s, it was brought here in 1884 probably from Coney Island and is ornately carved and brilliantly painted.

Under an arcade between a gaggle of souvenir shops and tearooms with outside umbrella-shaded tables, one can stroll back in time a hundred or more years, into Trinity Park, the central portion of the Wesleyan Grove Camp Meeting. Tempted by the warm sun and the silent surroundings, we sink onto a bench under tall shade trees. The open air tabernacle is directly ahead, setting for summer services and concerts. To our right is Trinity Methodist Church and all around the edge of the saucer-shaped park are tiny Carpenter Gothic houses, vying with each other for unique color and design. Since the lots they sit on were originally for tents, the houses are tall, narrow, and close to one another, seemingly in fellowship.

We stroll back to the harbor, passing by Wesley House, one of the few of the early hotels surviving. A bike shop housed in a tiny wooden building covered with wooden scrollwork shows the distinctive "Gingerbread" architecture of the camp ground spilled over onto secular establishments.

But, like the poet Robert Frost, we have miles to go before we sleep and so we are soon spinning along the beach road to the historic old whaling center of Edgartown. When Thomas Mayhew, Jr., established the first settlement here in 1642, he called it Great Harbour and it became a fishing and farming center. By the mid 1800's, whaling captains discovered that it indeed did have a great harbor and built extensive fleets and outfitting yards along its shores. They also built impressive mansions on the sloping hill surrounding it. As we walk the narrow, shaded streets lined with Greek Revival-style homes, we see essentially what those captains saw, for these remarkably beautiful structures have been well preserved.

We stroll up North Water Street past some of the finest three-story captains' houses, topped with widows' walks, decorated with fan-topped doorways, and surrounded by picket fences cascading with roses. We exclaim over these fences, which come in all sizes and are placed at every conceivable opportunity. Practically every resident we see is painting today. There must be an unwritten rule that Vineyarders spend each spring with a can of paint in one hand and a brush in the other!

Of course we must descend to the dock, browse in the gray-shingled art gallery and watch the tiny ferry shuttling cars, people, and bicycles back and forth across the channel to Chappaquiddick Island. The five-minute trip is accomplished by the busy little vessel *On Time III*, so called because, since there isn't a schedule, it is always on time!

A stroll back up Summer and Cook Streets takes us by the Dukes County Historical Society, repository for many unusual historical items, and the First Federated Church which still has a chandelier of original whale oil lamps. We step into the offices of one of the most famous weekly newspapers in America, the *Vineyard Gazette*, half hoping to see Henry Beetle Hough at the rolltop desk and the current collie at his feet. But we know the famous editor is now retired, so we leave him a note. A short walk later we stare up at the Giant Pagoda Tree, brought from China in a flower pot aboard a whale ship in 1837. It's the largest on this continent, according to the sign. A college age photographer is puzzling over how to fit this enormity into his viewfinder and finally settles for a closeup of the sign.

Regretfully we leave, promising ourselves a return visit soon, then continue up-Island through the rolling farmland. We are impressed by the well-used bicycle path that parallels the road and the pleasing green belt in between. We stop at the Place by the Wayside, a small pullout where a marker notes that it was here that Thomas Mayhew, Jr., often preached to the Indians. After he was lost at sea on a trip to England, the Indians placed stones at this spot in his memory. These were added to year by year and finally cemented together and a bronze marker added.

We pass through West Tisbury, a rural New England village where sheep once grazed on meadows and where wild grapes, succulent blueberries, and cranberry bogs are a reminder of earlier farms. The most potent reminder of the former days of cultivation are the endless stone walls which once bounded these farms. It's nice to know at least one former industry is still with us. The Chicama Vineyard is flourishing and its outstanding souvenir is a bottle of white Chardonnay wine, according to a recent issue of *Travel and Leisure* magazine.

The West Tisbury Congregational Church stands quietly watching over the village center with its town hall, formerly the Dukes County Academy building, and a general store that deals in everything. Traveling on to Chilmark, we stop at Beetlebung Corner to see the famous tupelo trees which the Vineyarders call "beetlebung," because its wood is so tough it can be used for mallets and as bungs—those plugs that fit into the holes of wooden casks, barrels, and boats. Too difficult to photograph, we decide, though many people try in the fall when scarlet leaves make this a grove of fire.

We continue up-Island into the narrow end of the land and the Indian town of Gay Head. The trees grow smaller, bent over permanently by the fierce, constant winds. Treeless dunes near the shore are covered with wind-sculptured shrubs as we near the world-famous clay cliffs, now a national landmark. We have seen them before, but our spirits lift in anticipation again. Climbing the sandy walk to the fenced-off observation point, we gaze at these multicolored wonders of nature. Those who know best say the most spectacular view of these cliffs is at sunset when the setting sun illumines the brick red, the tawny gold, and the blue-green strata. To my mind they are gorgeous anytime. Musing, I float back to the days when the earlier Wampanoags would gather clay in baskets to bring to vessels anchored offshore. Boston ships were a common sight here in the late 1800's as they waited for ferries to bring them the clay for city potters who turned out cannon moulds, pottery dishes, and fire bricks.

But this is a different era and visitors come not to take away clay but to gaze at these wonders. My reverie is abruptly broken by the arrival of a bus load of tourists. We chat with a winsome young couple from New York City who are on their honeymoon, and take a picture of them against the background of Martha's Vineyard's most important geological sight. From here there is a sweeping view of the Elizabeth Islands and of Nomans Land Island. With regret we leave the panorama and walk toward the cluster of Wampanoag Indian shops at the foot of the observation path. It's a pleasure to talk with Bertha Vanderhoop Giles, proprietor of the Stony Squaw Gifts, about the ancient lineage and history of her people, the Aquinnah group of Martha's Vineyard Indians.

The sun is beginning to descend and we must hasten on. Retracing our steps, we pause briefly to gaze across Squibnocket and Menemsha Ponds on this exceptionally clear day. Then down Cross Road to Menemsha, that incredible little capsuled fishing village—the last true picture of those that used to encircle the island. Fishing shacks are packed helter skelter along the inlet from the General Store to the Coast Guard Station. Lobster traps hang from every conceivable projection, perfect subjects for the photographer.

West Tisbury's outskirts are a collection of heterogeneous experiences. We slow to a crawl when we spot a family of gaily decked scarecrows presiding over a large garden. We stop to photograph father, mother, and baby swaying in the wind at the Littlefield gardens and discover that a recent postcard mailed from the mid-west addressed simply "Scarecrow Farm" reached its destination swiftly. Farther along is a magnificent oak, gnarled and hoary with age. Its intertwining branches form a natural umbrella. We pause in amazement, never having seen a tree like this anywhere. A delicious aroma floats across the road from a bakery, tempting us to stop for afternoon tea.

Except for the shoreline, West Tisbury does look like a town in the English midlands. Earlier folks thought so too and named it for Tisbury, England (not to be confused with our Tisbury which is known as Vineyard Haven).

Off again on our journey, we drive down a progressively more rutted Indian

Hill Road, for we are seeking out Christiantown. In 1659, Sachem Josias of Takemmy set aside this square mile as a township for new converts to Christianity, the Praying Indians. The only remaining structure is the minute Mayhew Chapel, so hidden by protective arches of the trees that we almost miss it. Peering through the windows we see six pews on each side of a central aisle and a massive, dark wooden pulpit. The Indian burial ground across the lane is almost as inconspicuous. Fieldstones are natural markers for the Indian graves which extend through the woods and over the hill. We wander for a time among the stones. The silence, broken only by the whisper of the leaves and the twitter of birds, seems a fitting background for a town that exists no more.

Returning to the Twentieth Century, we drive down-Island along the highway until we reach Lambert's Cove Road, where a short ride north reveals a crescent-shaped shore. Named for Jonathan Lambert, who became a landowner here in 1694, the sheltered cove was used as an anchorage by early settlers and by British privateers. In more recent times, troops have used these protected waters for practise maneuvers. Today the once busy settlement with its salt works, wharves and stores has relapsed into a quiet summer colony. Such notables as folk singer James Taylor, conductor Andre Previn, his actress wife Mia Farrow and journalist Katharine Graham of the Washington Post find relaxation here, along with the previously mentioned opera superstar Beverly Sills and many others.

We glance at the ferry schedule and our watches, then hurry to the highway, pausing only briefly on a small hill to gaze across the length of Tashmoo Lake, once a fresh water pond that is now open to the sea. Vineyard Haven, chief port of the island, is all business, in contrast to the sleepy countryside. After returning our rented car, we stroll through the bustling Main Street to the park. This sloping bit of green overlooking the harbor is named for William Barry Owen who made a fortune developing the gramaphone and headed the Victor Talking Machine Company. His spirit must feel quite at home on summer evenings when the band plays the familiar melodies. The D. A. R. Historical Museum is closed, so we content ourselves with peering through its windows. This old schoolhouse, built in 1828, is now educating in a different manner by displaying artifacts and pictures of Island history.

Seeking out Association Hall on Spring Street, we gaze at this seat of town government which upstairs houses the Katharine Cornell Theater. Nostalgically we recall meeting the famous actress, who spent many years on the island, part of the perennial theater colony. There is a vast number of creative people living here as we discover when we drop into the Bunch of Grapes Book Store on Main Street and browse at the table marked "Island Books." Many have been authored by residents who form a year-round literary colony that burgeons in the summer.

16

The hands of our watches are warning that departure time is coming and that ferries don't wait. We must still sample the island's clam chowder and freshly caught fish. Perhaps we'll top off our meal with homemade ice cream from that old-fashioned parlor with its multicolored and leaded Tiffany lamps.

Our final stop is at Seaman's Bethel, close by the ferry wharf. This branch of the Boston Seaman's Friend Society was once a bunkhouse and social center for sailors beached between sailings. Now it is filled with memorabilia of sailing and island life. We stand in awe before the intricate family tree of the Mayhews displayed on the wall and at the ships' logs and scrimshaw in the glass cases. More than one quiet moment is spent in the chapel. A luminous stained-glass window portrays Christ preaching from a boat, the deep blues of the sea and sky accented by the scarlet of His robe.

A growing hum outside alerts us to sailing time and we slip out the door and across the wharf. Lining up with the backpackers and bikers to go aboard, we watch the ferry disgorge its latest load. There are trailer trucks with building materials, station wagons with golf clubs and garden tools. Newcomers pass by rolling their suitcases on tiny wheels. One passenger carries a kayak paddle. The last car passes by, a symbol of all the rest. It is over-flowing with querulous children, harried parents, barking dogs, and scarlet geraniums, all about to fall under the island's spell.

III

WHAT WAS THIS ISLAND LIKE in the long ago? Who lived here before the great tourist invasion?

The written history of Martha's Vineyard began in 1524 when Giovanni da Verrazzano sailed by and may have landed, for he left a map of the coast off which this island, labelled Luisa, is plainly identifiable. Though many other ships must have sailed by, it was Bartholomew Gosnold's expedition for Sir Walter Raleigh in 1602 which left the next written record. John Brereton, one of the two scribes in Gosnold's party, kept a written "relation" of the trip, reporting on "the incredible store of vine and the beautie and delecacie of this sweet soile." Because of these prolific wild vineyards and in honor of his young daughter, Gosnold bestowed on the island its permanent name, Martha's Vineyard. The party had a pleasant stay for Brereton noted "we found our health and strength all the while we remained there to renew and increase." In the succeeding years until Pilgrim days, Samuel Champlain, Adrian Block, Thomas Hunt, and Thomas Dermer visited the island successively, some making a better impression than others on the native inhabitants.

These first white visitors found a large and economically stable native population living in permanent villages close to fresh water. About three thousand souls lived on this island which they called Noepe. These Wampanoags were divided into four large groups under leaders called Sachems. The Sachemship of Aquinnah comprised the present Gay Head, Takemmy was Tisbury, Nunpaug was in the Edgartown area, and the Chappaquiddicks came from the island so named today. The four hereditary Sachems and the Sagamores of each village gave allegiance to the Great Sachem Massasoit on the mainland and were part of the thirty or more tribute tribes that formed this rather loosely organized federation of southeastern New England native Americans.

The Vineyard natives fished, farmed, and hunted. Each family had its own land to cultivate, with corn the principal crop. Beans, squash, sunflowers, and Jerusalem artichokes were also grown. The many types of fish and game provided a varied diet. Seaworthy dug-out canoes aided in fishing and in occasional mainland visits. With cutting tools made from rocks, the natives fashioned soapstone bowls and many wooden articles. They also used clay from the colorful cliffs to make pottery utensils and vines to fashion baskets.

These Vineyard natives were innately hospitable, though they later became understandably suspicious and more aggressive after the infamous Thomas Hunt kidnapped a number of them and carried them off to Europe. One was Epinow who lived in England long enough to learn the language and judge correctly the nature of the greedy adventurers. He cleverly hinted that there was gold on Martha's Vineyard in great quantity. The bait worked and soon Epinow was sailing west on an expedition to the island commanded by a Captain Hobson and financed by the Earl of Southampton and Sir Fernando Gorges. When the vessel reached the harbor at the present-day Edgartown, Epinow jumped ship and the vessel returned to England empty "to the great dismay of Gorges and his collaborators."

After Thomas Mayhew purchased his parcel of islands for "a some of money" in 1641 from the English Lord, the Earl of Stirling, Sir Fernando Gorges made noises about his claim. Apparently Mayhew thought there was some validity to Gorges' claim, for he paid an additional "some" to Gorges, who styled himself Lord Palatine of the Province of Maine. Colonization began in 1642 when Thomas Mayhew, Jr., son and copatentee, brought over a few planters and established a settlement at Great Harbour, or the present Edgartown.

The Mayhew family, which from that time forth became an integral part of island history, was an interesting contrast in authority and servanthood. As Lloyd

Hare describes it in *Martha's Vineyard, A Short History and Guide:* "Only in the early history of Martha's Vineyard may one find a proprietory governor, or a succession of manorial lords or his Majesty's justices sitting in a bench in British dignity on one day and the next day walking twenty miles through uncut forests to preach the Gospel of Christ to the aborigines in wigwam or open field."

Relations between those first settlers and the Wampanoags were peaceful and courteous. The Mayhew party scrupulously observed native land titles, purchasing land in parcels as needed from the inhabitants. After the first houses were built and the soil tilled, the settlers established a democratic town government, set aside an acre for the dead on Burial Hill and erected a schoolhouse and a church. Thomas Mayhew, Jr., who was "a young gentleman of liberal education . . . having no small degree of Knowledge in Latin and Greek languages and being not wholly a Stranger to the Hebrew," was ordained pastor.

Mayhew wished passionately to share his faith with the natives, but they were not particularly interested, having a religion of their own. The spiritual world was very real to them. The Great Spirit, maker of mankind, was assisted by many lesser spirits, according to E. Gale Huntington writing in the aforementioned history guide published by the Dukes County Historical Society. "Indeed every object, animate and inanimate alike, had its spirit." All life was dependent on interlocking relationships, which is why the circle was and still is so important to native Americans.

One native, Hiacoomes, was very curious about the white man's God and soon came to the attention of Mayhew. The pastor invited Hiacoomes to his home and instructed him both in his faith and in the English language. In return, Hiacoomes taught him the native language. At first the other natives jeered at Hiacoomes. One scoffer asked Hiacoomes what he would do if any of his family fell sick, since the Wampanoags reckoned there were thirty-seven gods under the Great Spirit. "Shall I throw away these thirty-seven gods for one?" he questioned scornfully.

The eager Hiacoomes persisted, however, and by 1643 was educated sufficiently so his conversion was acknowledged. Together with Mayhew, Hiacoomes began spreading the gospel among his countrymen. By 1651 there were one hundred and ninety-nine men, women, and children who had embraced the English religion. That winter a school was opened for any natives wishing to learn. Eventually the number of natives professing Christianity reached 1,600. Rev. John Eliot, who was working with the natives on the Massachusetts mainland, heard of the Vineyard work and described it along with his own in a *Narrative of the Progress of the Gospel among Indians in New England.* When this was published in London, English philanthropists organized a Society for the

Propagation of the Gospel in New England which paid salaries to workers with the natives.

Meanwhile the elder Mayhew was as zealous in secular affairs as his son was in religious matters. From the first day he had striven to persuade the native leaders to agree of their own free will to English authority. By order of the crown of England, he expained, he was to govern the English settlers, but the Sachems and Sagamores would continue to govern their subjects. Religion and government were different, he said. Accepting the white man's God would not mean giving up authority over their subjects. As the Christian Indians increased in number, Mayhew urged the Sachems to add a few to their councils. In cases where Indians and English had disputes, Mayhew administered justice equally and the Sachems did the same. Governor Mayhew thus "charmed" the rulers, said an ancient sage "into an earnest desire to copy the English form of government."

About this time tragedy struck. Thomas Mayhew, Jr., who was thirty-seven years of age, embarked with about fifty other passengers for London to settle a family estate and to give English philanthropists a first-hand account of work with the natives. The ship, which carried a rich lading of goods and many people of importance, cleared Boston Harbor but was never heard from again. Governor Mayhew, though distraught by the death of his only son, picked up the missionary work, aided by his three grandsons and native leaders.

By 1670 "Praying Towns" were established on Nantucket and Martha's Vineyard. A fully organized church on the Vineyard was guided by the faithful Hiacoomes who had been chosen pastor. This unprepossessing native had blossomed into a strong leader, described by the poet Whittier as "the Forest Paul of his race." Hiacoomes' biography was published in Appleton's *Cyclopedia of American Biography* where he is listed among presidents, generals, and educators. John Tackanash was made teacher of the new parish. Later, when this first Wampanoag parish was divided, he was chosen pastor of the second native church. That these two Wampanoag divines were extremely successful is evidenced by comments in early records such as "Some of our Godly English People chearfully received the Lord's Supper administered by Tackanash."

Relations between English and Wampanoags were so satisfactory that, when the bloody King Philip's War broke out between natives and settlers on the mainland in 1675, the Martha's Vineyard Indians did not become involved. Instead they organized a military company for defense, some of whom were delegated to act as bodyguard for the governor. Church development continued unabated. Soon there was a large staff of Indian preachers, interpreters, and schoolmasters. Mayhew's English assistant was Peter Folger, later famous as the

20

maternal grandfather of Benjamin Franklin.

Change in the established ways came when Governor Mayhew died at "a great age wanting but six dayes of ninety years." In writing the news to Governor Thomas Hinckley of the Plymouth Colony, his grandson Matthew eulogized, "I got no great hope there will ever be the like in this selfish age." Grandsons Matthew and Thomas took over the civil administration of the island, while John tended the religious heritage. As a youth of twenty-one he had been ordained a pastor, serving the fledgling English settlements of Tisbury and Chilmark. John's son Experience followed in his father's footsteps, serving as pastor to natives and whites from 1693 to 1758. Like many literary Mayhews before and since, he authored several works both in English and in the native tongue. Experience's son Zachariah inherited the family's religious mantle when his brother Nathan, who was destined for the job, died two years after graduation from Harvard. However, Zachariah, it is recorded, did so reluctantly for he much preferred farming to preaching. Perhaps it was because he sensed the winds of change were blowing.

Up until this time the peaceful insularity of Martha's Vineyard had been protected not only by the friendly relations between people of two cultures, but also because of the abundance of natural resources. No need to venture off the island and thereby encourage outside influences when all of life's necessities and many of its luxuries were available at home. Only spices, sugar, tea, coffee, and rum were desired from overseas and these could be secured from passing vessels by barter or from the sale of produce on nearby mainland ports.

The first settlers had been amazed at the abundance of food on the island. They soon learned from friendly Wampanoags where and when to seek out the various fish and crustaceans. Salt ponds and streams had runs of alewives, perch and striped bass. Spring brought mackerel and great schools of scup which could be netted and trapped offshore. Flounder came close to the beaches in summer. Pollock was available spring and fall. Good sized haddock swam by in winter. Blackfish and lobster were caught year round. Thus there was plenty of protein to supplement the produce raised on the rolling farmland and the game caught in the woods.

Surprised at how like the Vineyard was to their homeland, these newcomers recalled the farming practices of their youth. They drained swamps, cleared land, dug ditches, and built miles of stone walls. "Wall-building bees" were held farm by farm so the back breaking work could be shared while the wives fed the hungry workers. That they did their work well is testified by the many sturdy walls remaining today. Large crops were planted and tended with wooden plows, harrows, and cultivators that can be seen in today's museums. Beans, squash, and corn were grown and laid by for the winter, along with marsh hay for the livestock. Flocks of sheep and cows grazed on the meadows, providing meat, butter, cheese, and milk. These herds also supplied enough wool and leather for clothing needs.

Despite the pleasantness of this little Eden, change was in the air and the times were unsettled. With the increase in population in all the colonies there were more frequent visitors from off-island. The villages increased as some stayed permanently. The newcomers brought new ideas and challenged the Mayhew government. Baptist and Methodist preachers arrived emphasizing new church ways and made inroads on both native and English (Congregational) parishes. The native population declined, partly because of disease brought by travelers and also because many had adopted English ways which were not as well suited to their constitutions. Then, too, every ship brought news of increasing tribulations being pressed upon colonists by King and Parliament. The Islanders were being urged with increasing fervor by loyalists and patriots to take sides as the seeds of the American Revolution were sprouting. All these ominous signs proclaimed that the first twelve decades of peace were coming to an end for the white and tan people on this placid island in the sea.

IV

BOATS AND VINEYARDERS seem to go hand in hand (or should we say hand in oar). From the time the Wampanoags hollowed out logs to make seaworthy canoes until the present, when the top-sail schooner *Shenandoah* reigns over other craft in Vineyard Haven Harbor, boats and ships have seemed like additional appendages to Islanders. This was especially true during the golden years of seafaring—the whaling era from 1780 to 1890.

Earliest boats of the English were square-ended, flat-bottomed scows. When pointed bows developed, they were referred to as "sharpies." As the native and English fishermen found there was better fishing offshore near undersea ledges, the No Mans Land boat was designed. Named for a small island off the Vineyard coast where the main base was established during the fishing season, these boats were "sharp at both ends, open fore and aft without curbing and had two masts which could be unstepped." These were small enough to be rowed by one man, yet were sturdy enough to ride out the heaviest gales. Boats varied in size from 16 to 28 feet and were soon copied up and down the East Coast.

Like their Wampanoag friends, the settlers first fished with primitive hooks and lines. When their farms produced flax in abundance, they used longer fishing lines and nets. Fish weirs, those ingenious arrangements of judiciously placed stakes and nets, made it possible to trap large schools of fish. Soon the yearly catch increased dramatically and barrels of salt cod and pickled herring were being exported to the mainland. By 1807, Edgartown Great Pond was yielding 1,000 barrels a year, and offshore fishing brought a much greater harvest.

This increased fishing activity made boat building one of the island's earliest trades. By the mid-1800's large vessels were sliding off the ways at Vineyard Haven, which never surrendered its prominence as the island's boat building headquarters. There was, of course, a similar rise in crafts and industries related to the ship building trade. Soon salt-makers, sail makers, coopers, blacksmiths, cordwainers (shoemakers), hatters, tanners, weavers, and furniture crafters were doing a brisk business around the harbors at Edgartown and Vineyard Haven and some were prospering in the smaller villages.

These same simple boats that in early years carried natives and settlers fishing also carried them out to harpoon the many whales disporting offshore. These huge leviathans were dragged ashore and their blubber "tried-out" in try works on the beach. "Whale cutters" were appointed by the towns as early as 1652 on the island. Noting that the resulting whale oil was much in demand on the mainland by both businesses and families for their oil lamps, a healthy export business began. When Vineyarders realized that there were whales larger than they had ever dreamed in deeper waters, they built larger ships to go after them. Edgartown and Vineyard Haven subsidiary industries and crafts increased in size and output again. By the time of the American Revolution there were twelve vessels in the island whaling fleet, and its sailors were venturing on longer and longer voyages. The golden era of whaling was about to begin.

Though the hostilities with England from 1775 to 1783 brought a temporary halt to whaling activities and most coastal trade, by 1791 the Vineyard vessels were rounding Cape Horn and chasing whales in the Pacific. For the next hundred years, except for temporary halts during the War of 1812 and the Civil War, the whalers of Martha's Vineyard ranged the seven seas on voyages that lasted sometimes three to five years. Ships were of necessity larger and sturdier to accommodate the increase in cargoes and crews.

This was the period of story and song that celebrated larger-than-life heroes and events as well as heart-rending tales of tragedy. Dionis C. and Sidney H. Riggs, in the aforementioned history and guide book, give a valuable account of those days. They refer to the saga of Captain George Fred Tilton who walked 3,000 miles across Arctic ice and the tip of Alaska to get help when nine whaleships were stranded in 1897. There are tales of mutiny and of shipwrecks. Happier stories recounted adventures of the ships *Splendid*, *Vineyard*, *Champion*, and *Pocahontas* which brought "wealth and homecoming young men back to the

23

island year after year." It was such tales that captured the imagination of Herman Melville, who wrote the great saga *Moby Dick*.

Something should be said about the captains, mates, and sailors who handled these great ships. Like the island they came from, these Vineyarders were sturdy and self-reliant. With intelligence and ingenuity they handled all types of responsibility. They went to sea at an early age and some were educated specifically for a sea career. Leavitt Thaxter, a Harvard graduate, ran a school in Edgartown where the most promising boys were sent for general education and navigational studies. Most of the graduates became officers not only of Vineyard ships but of others from eastern ports. The Dukes County Historical Society has a picture collection of one hundred whaling captains from Edgartown alone, which accounts for only a few of the Vineyard seamen. Captains were in complete charge of a vessel and men on the three-to-five-year voyage. They served as counselors, fathers, doctors, lawyers, and clergymen in addition to the main job as ship's captain. In foreign ports they were our country's first diplomats. Thus the name Martha's Vineyard was a familiar one in seaports around the world.

Logs of whaling ships are filled with human interest stories. When two ships from home met on whaling grounds, they "spoke" by setting signals. Then one captain would row to the other ship to "gam" or share the news. On one occasion a homesick young third mate from the Vineyard was overjoyed to see a special vessel sail into view while he was cruising in the Pacific. His heartfelt notation in the log reads, "Spoke to the *Luminary* and father came on board . . . glad was I to see him." There was a very special post office on the Charles Island in the Galapagos. Letters and well-worn copies of the *Vineyard Gazette* were left in a crude mailbox, for whalers often went there for huge turtles to vary shipboard diet.

In 1835 the Rev. Samuel Devens visited Martha's Vineyard and reported "out of a population in Edgartown of fifteen hundred (which number comprises all ages, male and female), about three hundred of those who have arrived at maturity—the most active and vigorous, the bone and muscle of the community, are, I may say, ever abroad and in all quarters of the globe: and further that, out of a population of three thousand on the Island, about five or six hundred cannot be said to have a home upon the land, but go down and not only go down, but live upon the sea in ships and do business, most venturesome business, in great waters."

Some of the travelers on the great waters were women, for often a captain would take his wife and family on these long voyages. In the book *Whaling Wives* by Whiting and Hough, there are stories about thirty-seven women who went to sea. Once two sea captains and their wives met in Paita, Peru, when the daughter of one was christened. Years later, they met again in West Tisbury at the wedding of the now grown girl. This one occasion symbolized the many friendships made by chance meetings in foreign ports.

While the largest ships were sailing the seven seas, Vineyarders were playing their part in the nearer waters on coastal packets and fishing vessels. They moved goods along the coast, operated ferries, and coped with the newer steamboats. These captains and their crew members were every bit as colorful as those who sailed the whalers. Their numbers were augmented by folks from foreign countries. Men from the Azores and Portugal had been recruited by whalers.

They, like the sure-footed and eagle-eyed Gay Head natives, were much in demand as harpooners and crewmen on the whaling vessels. Eventually many of these southern Europeans elected to remain permanently on the Vineyard. Thus names like Silva and Amaral were added to the voting roles along with the earlier English and Wampanoag names

We haven't said much about the wars, and there were several which put temporary dampers on marine activity. During the wars with England, the British navy watched for American ships. When captured, the seamen were given a choice of sailing the British ships or going to prison. Confederate ships were a hazard to Vineyarders during the War betwen the States. When the merchant fleet was forced into inactivity, the men who sailed its ships gave their services to their country. Edwin Coffin of Edgartown, for example, held a noncommissioned rating in the Federal navy. While serving on a warship off the Carolina coast, he was instrumental in saving the ship. The captain, knowing Coffin had captained a whaler, gave him the command when they were caught close to shore. Coffin brought the ship and its complement of 500 men safely clear of the shore and earned an official citation. Colorful stories of Vineyard men and their ships are legion and would fill countless books.

During the nineteenth century the waters around Martha's Vineyard were some of the heaviest traveled in the world. Sails of packet boats and fishing vessels were constantly parading on the horizon. Side wheelers paddled in passengers and freight. Steamers chugged in and out of the harbors. In the days before the macadam road and the motor car it was much easier to travel by sea than by land, and the marine activity along the coast proved it. On one single April day in 1889 there were anchored between West Chop and East Chop five tugs, fifty-four schooners, one brig, five barges, and many smaller craft. Some 60,000 sails passed by the island each year during the daylight hours.

But this golden age was coming to an end. The fishing grounds were yielding less and less fish. A well in Pennsylvania gushed up a quantity of oil which was to supplant that of the whale in the lives of Americans. The Cape Cod Canal, which was projected, would soon allow ships to go safely close to shore, avoiding more hazardous shipping lanes around the islands. Railroads were moving freight faster than ships. The Vineyarders' business was rapidly dwindling. The economy suffered for a time, but the island itself was saved. It remained much as it was, less changed than the neighboring mainland as the center of activity left the sea lanes. This was only for a short breathing space, however. Soon another onslaught was to threaten the insularity of Martha's Vineyard.

V

TOURISTS DISCOVERED THIS ISLAND early—exceedingly early if you count the first European explorers and the visiting mainland natives. Awashonks, female Sachem of the Sagkonets (located in part of today's Rhode Island), summered each year with her tribal members at Aquinnah (Gay Head) long before there were English settlements. Both Europeans and native Americans knew a good place to relax when they saw it and were forerunners of later hordes who by their very numbers threaten the isolation of the island.

The era of summer resorts as we know it began in the mid-1800's when overcrowded cities lost their rural flavor and there was a rush to mountains and seashore to escape summer heat. There were a few early "press agents" who touted the praised of Martha's Vineyard. Nathaniel Hawthorne spent most of the summer of 1835 on the island, writing about the sandy roads, the rolling gait of the townspeople and of his favorite way to reach the island. He preferred coming "by favor of the wind" as against traveling on a newfangled steamship which "tears her passage through the deep in spite of wind and tide, snorting and groaning as if tormented by the fire that rages in her entrails."

That same year a few Methodists chose a remote grove in the present day Oak Bluffs as a setting for their camp meetings and held a primitive gathering with a semicircle of nine tents improvised from sailcloth and a preacher's stand constructed from driftwood. From these tiny beginnings came the island's first major summer resort. Early attenders from the mainland brought home such glowing reports not only of conversions but of the island's beauty that the number of visitors soon increased. "I have attended forty camp meetings . . . but have never before seen so beautiful a spot for this sacred purpose" wrote one 1837 visitor. With testimonials like these, tents were soon replaced by little cottages, vessels brought visitors in greater numbers, and the annual gatherings at Cottage City— as the place was first called—were on their way to becoming the largest Camp Meeting in the world.

Politicians and sportsmen as well as the religious and literary people recognize the island's delights. Daniel Webster was an appreciative visitor in the impressive Edgartown mansion of Dr. Daniel Fisher in 1849. Less than a decade later, in 1858, a squadron from the New York Yacht Club sailed into Edgartown Harbor and remained overnight when bad weather threatened. Arranging an impromptu dance in the town hall, the sailors stayed long enough to "discover" the island. Their members have been regular visitors ever since, along with a steadily increasing number of skippers of all types of pleasure craft.

Soon more visitors arrived who were not involved with events at Cottage City, so hotels were built. The Oak Bluffs Land and Wharf Company owned three small inns, a wharf, and bathhouses. By 1872 the company had built the magnificent Sea View Hotel, unrivalled on the East Coast until fire destroyed it in 1892. The fame of the gorgeous Gay Head Cliffs drew tourists, who stayed with the lighthouse keeper or in private homes. As these visitors roamed the island, new hotels, guest houses, and homes sprang up.

A real estate boom swept the island. The Oak Bluffs Land Wharf Company advertised "Homes by the Seaside . . . one thousand lots for sale." This was the period when East Chop's Bellevue Heights began along with the Katama development at South Beach. Numerous others planned by Vineyarders and off-island speculators either saw the light of day or never made it off the drawing board. This period also saw new group developments. The Baptists held summer sessions for a time in Vineyard Highlands. An educational project, the Martha's Vineyard Summer Institute, forerunner of many later educational gatherings, held classes. It is said that this institute was the pattern for summer schools throughout the United States.

Bicyclists were delighted with the island since the rural lanes provided hours of pleasure. In 1887 the Massachusetts Division of the League of American Wheelmen held an annual conference. Riders delighted in wheeling their Rover bicycles along the smooth concrete avenues of Cottage City. A Boston syndicate formed the West Chop Land and Wharf Company. The Harbor View Inn at Edgartown was a favorite watering place of eastern seaboard families. In 1868, *Harper's Weekly* reported "These thousands of people who frequent Martha's Vineyard at this season have more and fresher pleasures than those who summer at Newport."

Among the famous visitors flocking to the island was President Ulysses S. Grant. In August of 1874 he was greeted by flags, bands, fireworks, and illuminated oriental lanterns at his arrival in Cottage City. After staying in one of the quaint cottages for the night, he attended the Camp Meeting's "Big Sunday" service, sitting on the platform among the preachers.

The Martha's Vineyard Camp Meeting was at its zenith, attracting twelve thousand visitors for "Big Sunday" which was in midsummer and climaxed each season. It is said that there were thirty-six prayer meetings in session this weekend and conversions were numbered in the hundreds. Trains had now arrived on the island and excursions brought visitors from all parts of the island, while special steamers disgorged boatloads incessantly. Boarding places and dining rooms as well as souvenir shops had sprung up around Cottage City. When the gradually encroaching secular resort came too close, a seven-foot picket fence was erected to protect worshippers from worldliness!

But the island had just been "discovered" by new multitudes, and the stream of tourists continued unabated. Most visitors stayed at least a few weeks or the entire summer, for life was lived at a slower pace then and the two-week summer vacation had not yet come into vogue across America. These visitors were oriented toward nature, enjoying the beaches, views, fishing, flowers, and birds. Pleasures were simple and family oriented. Some visitors—attracted first by the Camp Meetings, the educational sessions, or trips for business or sightseeing— were caught by the different atmosphere and decided to become residents. The list of eminent folks who have chosen Martha's Vineyard as a first or second home is endless. Professors, doctors, senators, writers, musicians fell under the island's spell. The opera star Nordica (of the Vineyard Nortons) was here. The author W. Somerset Maugham and Yale president Whitney Griswold found this a relaxing place. We don't dare begin to list the current stars who live here—from Vance Packard with his prolific pen to Beverly Sills, operatic superstar; from Joseph Allen, Yankee Oracle, to James Reston, New York journalist. But we must cease less we lay ourselves open to a charge of not naming others of importance.

Recent years have brought changes to our society—and the Vineyard has not escaped. The rich farmland fell into slumber when mammoth trucks arrived daily, stuffed with luscious vegetables and fruit for island consumption. The colorful lighthouse keepers departed when lights became automated. Electric generating plants gave up pulsating when it was cheaper to bring current in by cable from the mainland. No longer does a doctor in a top hat and flapping tails repair his phone lines on the way home from a house call. Now the telephone company handles all matters from a mainland office. The High School is regionalized. The Vineyard fleet of sturdy commercial fishing vessels expired in the 1950's, replaced by "factory" draggers berthed in mainland ports though fishermen still bring in lobsters, scallops, swordfish and cod. Planes swoop in and out of the skies with regularity, except when fog or storm interrupts the schedules. "You are still an island, depending on my whims" the weather seems to say.

Fortunately some things remain unchanged, unconquered by an invasion.

On winter evenings some folks enjoy eel stiffle for supper. As did the earlier Vineyarders, they dip into a dish featuring layers of eels, potatoes, and onions. Others enjoy kale soup, made with slices of spicy linguica, as did the first Portuguese whalemen here. The Wampanoags of Gay Head continue their tribal ways, part of mainstream America, yet also part of an ancient culture. They are proud that one of their number, Edwin D. Vanderhoop, was the first Indian to be elected to a seat in the Massachusetts legislature. Recently Beatrice Vanderhoop Gentry served on the Massachusetts Commission for Indian Affairs, the first all native Commission in 100 years.

Lobstering is still an important business in Menemsha and scalloping is still a favorite and rewarding activity. Town meeting is still held each year, as in the patriarchal Mayhew days, and every resident has his or her say. The island is still turning out captains, though some are of a different vintage than in the old days. "Learn to Sail—Go Home a Captain" says an advertisement in the *Vineyard Gazette*, "We present you a diploma after completing our lessons." Also the beach plums still burst in white beauty from unpromising, twisted black bushes each spring and the swamp maples turn a riot of color every fall. All the other marvelous occurrences in the calendar of nature return unerringly each season— even an occasional hurricane.

Today there are six towns on the island, according to the masthead of the 133-year-old *Vineyard Gazette:* Edgartown, Oak Bluffs, Tisbury (Vineyard Haven), West Tisbury, Chilmark, and Gay Head. According to the Martha's Vineyard Commission, winter population is approximately 8,000 and summer folk bring it to 52,000. All of the winter people, and most of the summer folk, too, are concerned over the worrisome specter of too many people overrunning a too small island. Conservation and ecology are often-used words.

Some folks have backed up their concern with action, illustrating how sometimes one small step can lead to a giant stride. In 1959, Henry and Betty Hough gave a tract of their own land containing a pond, a knoll, and some pleasing vistas to an organization founded by themselves, the Sheriff's Meadow Foundation, Incorporated. The purpose of the new corporation was "to preserve, administer, and maintain natural habitats for wild life on Martha's Vineyard for educational purposes and in the interests of conservation." Other land was added to this by similarly concerned citizens. Now the foundation owns over 750 acres which reveal all aspects of island terrain: upland, shore, woodland, marshes, ponds, and brooks. Because of such efforts on the part of citizens and government, there are now twelve conservation areas, comprising some 5,000 acres, which will be preserved forever in their natural state. Many can be enjoyed by the public.

A study by the National Park Service in 1964 warned of blight and tasteless commercial exploitation if some controls were not adopted. Another study commissioned by the county in 1969 led to more talk, and some controversy. The Nantucket Sound Islands Trust, introduced in the United States Senate by Senator Edward Kennedy in 1972, generated further talk and more controversy. Now the state has established a regional planning agency and residents are attacking the dilemma again. A Department of the Interior report capsuled the problem cleverly when it said, "All preservation is obviously wrong, but all expansion is worse!"

Meantime, and fortunately, there are families with large land holdings who are dedicated to preservation rather than development. When the former first lady, Jacqueline Kennedy Onassis purchased a 375-acre tract at Gay Head from the Hornblower family in 1978, her attorney revealed she had pledged to keep "this irreplaceable fragment of a vanishing island" (according to a mainland editorial) close to its pristine state and continue it as a wildlife sanctuary.

About this time, a substantial plot of land including an ancient burial ground at Gay Head was deeded to the Wampanoags of Gay Head, by the Strock family further increasing the natural acreage.

With evidence of such concern, might we dare hope that this island's people, customs, and vistas will remain set apart, insulated, influenced but never overcome by succeeding invasions?

In the June 1977 *National Geographic Magazine*, Kenneth MacLeish writes, "There are places on our planet destined by their form and their location to stir emotions of man . . . they have this in common: they are essentially different from all that surrounds them, they are special, therefore wonderful." He was talking specifically about Mont Saint Michel off the coast of France, but we can imagine Vineyarders nodding in agreement, picturing their own small island off the coast of America. We imagine, too, that many an off-islander, entranced by Martha's Vineyard's moors and dunes, shares the longing expressed by the poet Lucy Bull in her "Ballade of Islands":

> "I would I had been Island-born,
> I dearly love things insular."

THE PLATES

A WARNING LIGHT AT EAST CHOP

Atop a high bluff stands East Chop Lighthouse, warning ships to stay clear of its rocky base as they enter Vineyard Haven Harbor. The lighthouse stands on what Governor Thomas Mayhew referred to in 1644 as "the easternmost chop of Holmes Hole" (Vineyard Haven's earlier name).

In 1869 Captain Silas Daggett, conscious of the need for a beacon, built a lighthouse here, paying for it out of his own pocket. Then in 1871 the lighthouse burned completely when one of the ladies who cleaned it used gasoline too near a briskly burning stove. Undaunted, Captain Daggett rebuilt the structure in 1872. Finally in 1876 the government took over ownership and the following year erected a new iron tower.

This high hill with its spectacular view was used earlier for signals of another sort. Jonathan Grout built a signal tower here in 1802 as part of a semaphore telegraph system. Using additional towers in Nantucket, Chappaquiddick, Falmouth, and on up the Massachusetts coast, Grout kept Boston ship owners advised of their arriving vessels.

Originally called "The Highlands," the community clustered near the lighthouse is now part of Oak Bluffs. Settled as a summer resort, it once boasted an elegant hotel with sixty rooms, a large wharf that accommodated steamboats, and the first summer school for teachers in America. The Martha's Vineyard Summer Institute was established here in 1878 by a group of educatiors who were inspired by the work of Louis Agassiz on nearby Penikese Island. In its most flourishing years, as many as 800 folks attended, wishing to combine "the study of some specialty with the rest and recreation of a delightful seaside resort." When mainland colleges and normal schools began offering academic credit for summer courses, interest declined, causing the closing of the Institute in 1907. This community also was once the site of a Baptist Camp Meeting. Though these educational and religious organizations no longer exist, the summer resort flavor still remains.

A "BRIDGE" TO THE VINEYARD

Boats from Hyannis, Falmouth Inner Harbor, Woods Hole, and New Bedford are "bridges" to the Island, bringing passengers and bicycles in the milder weather. This ferry bringing eager visitors into Oak Bluffs harbor is a familiar sight, particularly in summer.

When the passengers disembark, they find a charming little resort community that began in 1835 with a religious camp meeting. First called Cottage City, it grew and grew as "support" industries like dining rooms and rooming houses provided for the comforts of the faithful. On February 17, 1880, the governor of Massachusetts made Cottage City a separate town with a stroke of his pen. No longer did the year-round and summer residents have to pay taxes to Edgartown, but could arrange their own destiny. In 1907 the name of the town was changed to Oak Bluffs, which originally had been the name of the area's first development company.

Oak Bluffs also was the scene of one of the Island's greatest undertakings. In 1874 the Martha's Vineyard Railroad was launched, linking Oak Bluffs with Edgartown, Katama, and South Beach. The railroad was eventually succeeded by an electric trolley line which connected Oak Bluffs to Vineyard Haven. This mode of transportation disappeared with the age of the automobile.

One of the joyous occasions during the railroad era was the visit of President Ulysses S. Grant, whose distinguished party included Vice-President Wilson, Secretary of State Robeson, Postmaster General Jewel, and Governor Talbot of Massachusetts.

34

THE LACE VALENTINES OF COTTAGE CITY

Visitors often wander bemused among the tiny, rainbowhued cottages of the Wesleyan Grove Camp Meeting in Oak Bluffs. There are gables, turrets, spires, scrollwork, and lacy designs ad infinitum. Leaded glass windows with intricate tracery and Gothic revival architecture add an unusual touch while a riot of flowers spilling out of window boxes and overflowing the wee gardens add color in the warm months.

"Reformation" John Adams, an itinerant Methodist preacher assigned to the Island in 1821-1822 and again in 1826-1827, is credited with beginning the Camp Meeting movement on the Island. He is said to have preached and prayed with such extraordinary zeal that he made many converts both from the unchurched and the established Congregational parishes. As early as 1827 he held a camp meeting at West Chop. Then one of his devoted followers, Jeremiah Pease, found the ideal site for the present Camp Meeting under a grove of stately oaks. At the first gathering held the summer of 1835, nine tents housed the worshippers and services were held in the open air. By 1857 sixty ministers attended summer Camp Meeting and by the following year 12,000 people came. The first wooden house was built in 1897 by Perez Mason who also planned the mammoth canvas-topped Tabernacle. In 1897 the present majestic open-aired, iron Tabernacle was built and quaint wooden cottages had replaced tents. These "lace valentines," of which some 300 survive, gave the first name of Cottage City to the little town.

The Camp Meeting is still very much a part of the Martha's Vineyard summer scene. In addition to services, classes, community sings, concerts, and lectures, there is an annual "Grand Illumination" when, during a band concert, oriental lanterns are simultaneously lighted throughout the community.Hung from porches, trees, and lines crisscrossing Trinity Circle, these cause a heartfelt "oh" from the waiting crowd. One enthusiast in earlier days observed this "resembled the celestial city's pearly gates, whose translucence would manifest the beauty of the glorious light within."

CARS AS WELL AS PEOPLE DISEMBARK AT OAK BLUFFS

Ferries which carry cars and trucks, as well as people and bicycles, also put in at Oak Bluffs, though not as often as at Vineyard Haven. Like most resorts, the surroundings are ever changing. Since this picture was snapped a bank has been added to the scene and the ebb and flow of human activity continues as inexorably as that of the tides.

A short distance to the left is a small green with a Civil War statue and monument. Unlike most in the country, the monument is dedicated to soldiers on both sides of the War between the States, and may be the only one memorializing Confederates north of the Mason-Dixon line. It was erected in 1892 at the instigation of Charles Strahan, a former Confederate soldier and for a time editor of the now defunct *Martha's Vineyard Herald*. He had served in Company B of the 21st Virginia Regiment. Presumably feelings had become less violent in the thirty years following the war and residents could be magnanimous to earlier enemies.

From this point it is an easy walk through the east side of the bustling Circuit Avenue. Here are several historic sites not related to the early Methodists. On Grove Avenue is the eight-sided interdenominational Union Chapel which was built "to provide persons of different creeds and beliefs, but a common belief in God" to worship. Designed by Samuel Pratt it was erected in 1871. Baptists wanted their own place and in 1878 built a small church on the corner of Grove Avenue and Cottager's Corner. Now the Bethel Apostolic Church, it served as the Town Hall for Oak Bluffs residents until the new one was erected near the wharf.

SETTING SAIL FROM EDGARTOWN HARBOR

This schooner cruising the waters of the Vineyard is a reminder of the profusion of sails once seen just off the Island in past centuries. Barques, barkentines, packets, privateers, whalers, ferries, and sloops carried sailors and passengers on countless trips to the mainland and other island ports. This fragile communication chain was the only means of contact for many decades and was easily broken by the fierce and erratic New England weather.

The excellent harbor at Vineyard Haven was known from earliest days as a port of refuge in stormy·weather. Not all the sails which appeared heralded friendly folk. The British were well aware of this fine harbor and sailed in often during both the American Revolution and the War of 1812. Residents close to shore were often harried by foraging parties who took sheep, cattle, fowl, and gunpowder to provision English troops.

Probably the most famous, or should we say infamous, foragers were those under the command of Major General Earl Gray in 1778. During Gray's Raid the foraging party gathered so much stock there was little left for Vineyarders, though tales are told of how the doughty islanders, alerted by lookouts, concealed many sheep, cattle, pigs, and poultry in swamps and woods. That the raiders ventured far across the Island is confirmed by their whirlwind visit to Chilmark. Here in 1778 they relieved tax collector Elijah Smith of 390 pounds in tax receipts.

During this period all able-bodied men and older boys were either manning ships or fighting in the war, so the courageous Vineyarders who opposed these forays were largely old men, women, and children. At the Daughters of the American Revolution Museum in Vineyard Haven is a reminder of such bravery. In 1776, during the Revolution, three young girls blew up the town's Liberty Pole, rather than have it used by the British as a spar for one of their warships.

SPINNAKER CONTEST DURING RACE WEEK

Each July, Race Week in Edgartown is a highlight of the summer season. Receptions, balls, and many other social events complement the actual races which include events for all classes.

In 1978 the prestigious Edgartown Yacht Club held its 55th annual regatta in connection with Race Week. The opening event of what was billed as "the premier deep water racing program on the East Coast" was the 205-mile-long Vineyard Ocean Triangle Race. About 200 ocean racers left Edgartown on the prescribed course, which took them to a point southeast of Block Island and another near the Nantucket Shoals before they headed homeward toward Buzzards Light Tower and the finish line off Edgartown Lighthouse. Trophy races for cruising class yachts and shorter events for all other categories challenged skippers and brought additional throngs to swell further the already burgeoning summer population.

The New York Yacht Club was the earliest yacht club on the Island, maintaining summer headquarters at New York Wharf, which was located on the present road toward East Chop from Vineyard Haven. The first Island yacht club was formed in 1903, a forerunner of the present Edgartown Yacht Club. The Vineyard Haven Yacht Club was founded in 1928.

The headquarters of the Edgartown Yacht Club is at the very end of Main Street on the site of Osborne's Wharf in whaling days. Samuel Osborne, Jr., for whom it was named, was reputed to be at one time the largest single owner of whale ships in the entire country. Today the Club regularly conducts summer-long racing programs and sailing lessons.

ART GALLERY OVERLOOKS TOWN DOCK

The Old Sculpin Gallery that is filled with artistic creations to tempt one's pocketbook, once held treasures of another kind. Manuel Swartz, boat builder par excellence, turned out graceful gaff-rigged catboats in the early part of this century. His products were much sought after for fishing and sailing. When postwar years brought fiberglass hulls and newer, faster designs, the popularity of his boats declined. Swartz also built and operated the Chappaquiddick ferry. During this period he added the tower to his boat shop.

Folks who wait for today's ferry can browse in the art gallery or sit on the double-decker dock in the sunshine. If they doze a bit during this unexpected siesta, they can easily dream of the previous century when at the original large wharf whale ships were unloading their cargoes, coastal schooners were bringing in lumber, coal, and other necessities, while paddle steamers disgorged passengers from the mainland. From the surrounding harbor in those days rose a hum and bustle of supporting business establishments. Riggers, caulkers, coopers, sail makers, blacksmiths, shopkeepers, and artisans created an obbligato for the forceful shouts of ship's officers.

A strong blast from a passing yacht will call these waiting passengers back to the present and to the incoming ferry. Visitors here on Memorial Day realize the town has not forgotten its maritime heritage. Town dock is the site of impressive ceremonies when school children toss flowers into the harbor as a memorial to Islanders who have been lost at sea.

44

SHUTTLE TO CHAPPAQUIDDICK ISLAND

Threading its way through marine traffic is the busy little ferry *On Time III* which makes countless trips each year between the docks at Edgartown and Chappaquiddick. It shuttles back and forth energetically each day until midnight in summer and until 6 PM off season. We observed it at near capacity carrying two cars, two bicycles, and seven passengers. Those who missed it were content to wait in the warm sunshine since the next trip was only minutes away.

Prior to 1934, when a ferry was necessary, a small power boat towed a barge with a capacity of one car. Then Manuel Swartz, local shipbuilder, and Anthony Bettencourt designed the first self-powered ferry, calling it the City of Chappaquiddick. Though less than 40 feet long, it doubled the capacity, having space for two cars.

The first *On Time,* a diesel ferry, made its debut in 1948. It was so christened because it was always on time, there being no schedule. *On Time II* began its duty in 1969 and *On Time III* in 1973. Each was a bit larger than the last, but even so, the current ferry can probably vie with any other on the East Coast for the title of the country's smallest ferry.

LOBSTERING EXPEDITION

A small vessel towing lobster traps is a familiar sight on Martha's Vineyard shores. Soon to be set into the sea, these traps will provide succulent morsels to satisfy residents and visitors.

In the background is Dyke Bridge which spans an inlet from Cape Pogue Bay. North over the bridge is Cape Pogue Light, built in 1801. Along the eastern stretch of dunes and beach is the Wasque Wildlife Preservation. Though no cars are allowed here, the public is invited to enjoy the area which abounds in scrub oak, pine, and beach plum bushes. To the south is the barrier beach which at times stretches unbroken to the Vineyard and at other times is broken by angry seas surging into Katama Bay.

Highest point on Chappaquiddick Island is Sampson's Hill. From here pilots watched for incoming ships, then sailed out to meet them and guide the vessels safely into harbor. In 1830 a flagstaff and signal marked this crest. Then in 1845 these were replaced by the semaphore station, which was part of the message service transmitting news of approaching vessels to Boston via Nantucket, East Chop, and Falmouth stations.

Chappaquiddick, which means "refuge island" in the Wampanoag's tongue, was one of the four original sachemships on Martha's Vineyard when Governor Thomas Mayhew's party arrived. The Indian leader was Sachem Pahkehpunnassoo, who arranged with the governor for the settlers to have grazing rights. White settlement on Chappaquiddick began in the mid-1800's and concentrated in the southern section, while the Indian inhabitants clustered mostly in the north.

Though land development fever hit the Vineyard in the 1860's and spread to Chappaquiddick by 1890, the proposed building schemes were not carried through. Now the landowners are dedicated to preserving the Island's beauty and to protecting it from commercialism.

48

EDGARTOWN VIEWED FROM CHAPPAQUIDDICK

Outgrowth of the first tentative English settlement in 1642, Edgartown is seen today in substantial splendor framed in the deep blue of ocean and sky. The town was so named in 1671 for Edgar, the infant son of the Duke of York, who was heir presumptive to the British throne. A tiny settlement for the first few decades, Edgartown rapidly sprang into worldwide predominance when its whalers roamed the globe.

On the right in the distance can be seen some of the elegant captains' houses built by the masters of these whaling ships. The imposing mansions, many topped with widow's walks and of Greek Revival style, make this one of New England's lovelier towns. In the foreground and at the left a variety of boats can be identified serving both pleasure and business interests.

A walking tour is a delightful way to experience a step back into yesterday, for the town is much as it was during its nineteenth century heyday. This shire town for Dukes County has the church with the earliest ecclesiastical roots, as symbolized by the white steeple seen poking its way through the greenery at left. Here also is the Dukes County Historical Society repository for many artifacts, early literature, and Island history. Just a stone's throw away is the venerable, shingled home of the *Vineyard Gazette* and Four Corners, heart of the business district. A short walk up North Water Street brings one to the Daggett House Inn built in 1750 for whaling captain Timothy Daggett. It has been successively a store, a sailor's boarding house, and a counting house during whaling days before becoming an inn.

STATELY OLD CAPTAIN'S HOUSE FACES THE SEA

When the whaling captains' fortunes grew, these newly wealthy merchants built imposing mansions overlooking the harbors and the sea. One of the most photographed is this three-story Bliss House on North Water Street in Edgartown. It was built in 1832 and purchased by Captain Jared Fisher. He married into the Bliss family whose descendants have lived here since.

This particular street is noted for its magnificent captains' homes. Fanlights, widow's walks, fancy scrollwork, and carvings are a delight to the eye. It is especially interesting to stroll the brick walks at dusk when the soft light from houses' interiors give a long ago aura.

Vineyard Haven has its historic homes too, though not as many. A great fire swept through that town on August 11, 1883, and destroyed over 60 houses. One of those that escaped the blaze is the Ritter House on Beach Street, which has been placed on the National Register of Historic Places. The Ritter House was built in 1796 by Jireh Luce. Of simple Federal style, it once served as an inn as well as a home to many prominent citizens.

Other Vineyard Haven homes with an earlier flavor may be found on William Street in the historic district.

SOCIAL ARBITER PREFERS SIMPLE LIFE

Emily Post, noted judge of the social life, traveled in the highest circles of society and handed down decisions on the proper actions to the beautiful people decades ago. Yet, when she relaxed, it was at this simple two-story frame house on Fuller Street in Edgartown. The profusion of colorful blossoms are reminiscent of those which graced the tables of leaders of high society, while the widow's walk makes a transition to island life. These roof promenades were constructed so the waiting women could watch for their menfolk's returning ships. One wag commented recently that he thought widow's walks were wrongly named, since widows no longer needed to scan the horizon for a homecoming husband!

It is fascinating to note that Emily Post was first known as an author of novels with European settings; but, when she published *Etiquette* in 1922, she became more widely known as an arbiter of manners. In 1932 she began a syndicated newspaper column about etiquette and related problems which continued her popularity for many years.

METHODIST CHURCH BUILT BY WHALING CAPTAINS

This fourth building to house the Methodist congregation in Edgartown was dedicated in 1843. Financed almost entirely by whaling captains, it is of neo-Greek design by Frederick Baylies, Jr., the son of the last missionary to the Indians. Baylies also designed three other churches as well as many classic style homes. The lumber for this church was brought from Maine by ship by Captain John O. Morse. Built to seat 800 and with a tower 92 feet high, it is a welcome sight to homecoming sailors. The tower clock was given in 1889 as a memorial to Captain Chase Pease by his grandson Charles Darrow.

The congregation's first home was the tiny appendage to the Captain Chase Pease home on Main Street. The second church building once stood on Winter Street but was cut in sections and reconstructed on Middle Road in Chilmark in 1827. The third Methodist building was the current Edgartown Town Hall which was erected in 1828.

Next door to the present church is the handsome mansion built in 1840 for Dr. Daniel Fisher, an energetic soul who made quite an impact on the Island. Dr. Fisher arrived in 1824 to practice medicine and five years later married Grace Coffin, daughter of a prominent Edgartown merchant and ship owner. His interests expanded beyond medicine to include a whale-oil refinery that supplied lighthouses all over the country, a large spermaceti candle factory, and several whaling ships. He was founder and first president of the Martha's Vineyard National Bank.

Close by is St. Elizabeth's Catholic Church, a beautiful modern structure. St. Andrew's Episcopal Church with its stained-glass Tiffany windows can also be seen.

GARLANDED FENCES AND WHITE CLAPBOARDED HOUSES

Quaint white clapboard cottages surrounded by picket fences and garlanded with flowers are a common sight on the Vineyard. These create an uncommonly pleasant atmosphere for walking or bicycling. A car driver is apt to miss too much. This Davis Lane corner is in the center of an interesting walking tour.

Close by on this fascinating tour once can see the weathered, shingled home of the *Vineyard Gazette* (not pictured). Founded in 1846, the paper has been edited and printed in this building since 1938. Edgar Marchant came to the Vineyard at the age of thirty-two to start a paper that would not just cover local news but which would "furnish the latest news both foreign and domestic" as well as to provide moral and religious reading. Since whaling was at its peak then, reports from Lahina in the "Sandwich Islands," the Azores, and other world ports were a common occurrence. Henry Beetle Hough and his late wife came to the Vineyard in 1920 to edit the weekly and under their direction it became legendary among professional journalists. James Reston, New York journalist, and his his wife Sally Fuller Reston, bought the paper in the 1960's. Though Henry Beetle Hough is still listed on the masthead as editor, he is retired and hopefully adding to his considerable number of books about Martha's Vineyard.

The interesting old Gazette building was erected before the Revolution and once served as the town poorhouse. It is known as the Captain Benjamin Smith House. Smith, who was a captain in the Island militia, was instrumental in capturing British vessels during two naval engagements.

FEDERATED CHURCH HAS ANCIENT ROOTS

The beginnings of this congregation coincide with the arrival of Thomas Mayhew, Jr., in 1642. This orthodox (Congregational) parish of the first settlers had offshoots with the passage of time, such as the lovely meetinghouse of the old Congregational Church in West Tisbury. But the original parish remained and flourished as a Congregational parish until 1925. At that time the Baptist Church had become the Masonic Hall. So the Baptist Church, which had been founded by Rev. William Hubbard in 1823, merged with the Congregational to become the Federated Church. Thus, though a relatively new organization, it has an exceedingly distinguished past.

The present edifice was erected in 1828 and designed by the earlier mentioned Frederick Baylies, Jr. The interior still has a long ago air with its box pews, one of the earliest Ingraham clocks, and a chandelier with original whale-oil lamps.

Today the Island has at least two dozen churches of various denominations. Three Episcopal, three Roman Catholic, a Unitarian-Universalist, a Hebrew Center, and a Christian Science Society are listed in the *Visitor's Guide* of the Martha's Vineyard Chamber of Commerce. Along with several other more recent religious groups, these have joined the earliest Congregational, Methodist, and Baptist parishes.

FRESNEL LENS STILL SHINES

On the lawn of the Dukes County Historical Society in Edgartown stands a brick tower holding an unusual historical treasure. A Fresnel lens, invented by Augustin Fresnel in 1854, was constructed by the Henry Lapaute Company, winning a gold medal at the 1855 Paris Exposition. Purchased for sixteen thousand dollars, the lens was brought to Gay Head and installed in the new steel tower. The unique light, which first shone over Nantucket Sound on December 1, 1856, had 1,008 prisms and an apparatus for revolving them. It made quite an impression for, in *Harper's Magazine* the following year, General David Hunter Strother noted "Of all the heavenly phenomena I have had the good fortune to witness . . . I have never seen anything that, in mystic splendor, equalled this trick of the magic lantern at Gay Head." When electricity and more powerful bull's-eye lights were secured in 1951, the famous Fresnel lens was retired. Today on some summer evenings its unique light is demonstrated to the delight of tourists.

The attractive grounds at the historical society also feature a colonial herb garden and a carriage shed housing a whaleboat, old carriages, sleds, and a headlight from the Martha's Vineyard railroad engine. On a lighter note, visitors can also see two marble gravestones for Nancy Luce's pet chickens!

The museum-library records the history of man's existence on Martha's Vineyard from the very earliest natives to the current tourist scene, as well as paintings by Thomas Hart Benson. The complex also includes the Thomas Cooke House, built in 1765, which houses many historical exhibits. Thomas Cooke was a leading citizen of the day, having served as Edgartown's Collector of Customs, Justice of the Peace, and in other public offices. Thus it seems fitting that the contents of his house portray the life of the Vineyard through the years.

UNLOADING SWORDFISH AT EDGARTOWN

Amid the pristine pleasure craft in the crowded harbor are the fishing boats, workhorses of the maritime fleet. These provide fish for Island tables as well as for coastal markets. Hardworking fishermen leave the Vineyard harbors in late afternoon, travel through the night, and arrive at Georges Bank by dawn. This fishing ground, equal to any bread baskets on land, has an amazing proportion of the edible fish of the world.

According to John H. Mitchell, writing in a Massachusetts Audubon Society letter, Georges Bank is a very busy part of our planet. "Approaching at night across the unfished portion of Atlantic between Nantucket and the Bank is like coming upon some well lit city. The lights of draggers, processing ships, and research vessels flash on the horizon, and radar screens are crowded with moving dots. The image is complicated in early fall by the presence of land creatures. Moths, monarch butterflies, flickers, warblers, and other migratory birds periodically appear and disappear over the horizon."

There is much concern that oil drilling on Georges Bank might ruin these vast fishing grounds. As Representative Gerry Studds declared recently in a major speech, "Our revitalized fisheries should flourish long after any oil boom has busted." So folks are watching the activity offshore and the legislation on land, since fish are a renewable resource which is not true of oil.

SUNBATHING AT SOUTH BEACH

A seemingly endless stretch of sand forms the main base of the triangle that is Martha's Vineyard and is the mecca for sunbathers in season. The azure sky lightly strewn with wispy clouds, and the deeper blue ocean framed by golden sand is the scene most folks picture when a Martha's Vineyard summer comes to mind. This perfect place for swimming and drowsing is also ideal for beachcombing since the waves are constantly tossing treasures onto the shores. Once in a great while people do find cloudy glass bottles with hardly legible messages inside, but most often they settle for a variety of shells. Too often they must step around plastic, cans, and other debris of modern life.

But it is not always summer at South Beach. When colder days of fall and winter come the ocean continues to roll and the sands shift unceasingly. The muffled roar is unending as water, sand and pebbles grate and grind. When storms come the beach grasses huddle low in the dunes while the driving rain and the furious winds lash the shore. After the tempest subsides and the beachcombers venture forth again, they find new treasures, like lobster-pot buoys torn from their moorings. Their bright, painted surfaces make colorful decorations when clustered on the side of a weather-beaten house. Other finds are fragments of glass, sharp places rounded by the sea and sand, which make rainbow centerpieces in a glass bowl.

PLACID PARSONAGE POND

Parsonage Pond in West Tisbury is a placid home for a variety of species of wild life. Most of the year the surroundings are quiet, but when winter comes there is activity aplenty. This body of water freezes over early and is a favorite spot for ice skating. Whenever the temperature dips, boys and girls and even oldsters can be seen swirling, dipping and even sometimes falling on the ice.

A short distance away is Old Mill Pond, known locally as Swan Pond because of its perennial swan family. This body of water is peacefully placid too, giving no hint of the industrial activity that took place in earlier decades when folks were drawn to this spot because there was no stream in Edgartown strong enough to power a waterwheel.

James Allen, James Skiffe, Jr., William Pabodie, and Josiah Standish (son of Miles) were the earliest proprietors when the settlement began here about 1668. Since those early days the Mill Pond shore has been the setting for several industries. There were at various times gristmills, a carding mill, a short-lived flour mill, and a furniture factory. A woolen factory produced "kerseys and satinets" for about 100 years. One of the gristmills was erected in 1665 by the famous Indian fighter Captain Benjamin Church. Joseph Merry bought the gristmill from him when Captain Church left to fight in King Philip's War. Nantucketer Tristram Coffin, whose son John lived in Edgartown, owned it for a time. Thomas Look bought out the Coffin family in 1715 and the Looks ran the mill until it was discontinued and removed in 1877.

Mill Pond is near the typical New England village of West Tisbury, with its white steepled church, post office, and town hall. There is also a Youth Hostel close by and the privately-owned Joshua Slocum House. Captain Slocum wrote about his own incredible adventures in the book *Sailing Along around the World*.

CONTINUING AN ANCIENT OCCUPATION

Though few and far between, there are some working farms left on the Island. A few sheep, some Black Angus cattle, and a horse or two add a pastoral touch to the upland meadows which are so reminiscent of the winding lanes and peaceful pastures of England. Among the produce of today can still be found corn, which was a staple for the native population and the first English colonists over three hundred years ago.

A visiting English lady confirmed some years back the likeness of Martha's Vineyard to England. The daughter of the noted English composer Sir Edward Elgar, Mrs. Carice Elgar Blake, noted that she felt drawn to the Island because the up-Island moors reminded her of the midlands in her native country "with their gray-blueness and rocks scattered here and there . . . an occasional thistle and always the sea at hand."

But there are more than one or two horses. On closer examination we find there must be a multitude of horse lovers since there are an unusually large number of riding stables considering the size of the year-round population. Some offer trail rides through the pastureland and State Forest. Others arrange for group and individual riding lessons—either western or English style. For the real enthusiasts there are horse shows. A few are open to the public for a small fee, while others are "schooling" shows limited to students. Some of the largest shows are found at the fair grounds in West Tisbury.

LOOKING WEST FROM WEQUOBSQUE CLIFFS

South Beach gradually turns into bouldery clay cliffs as one travels up-Island along the shore. Looking further west toward Squibnocket Point, one can pick up the trail of the Montauk Till. This is the term geologists give to the till left by the Buzzards Bay Lobe of the glacier during the Ice Age. The weight of the glacier squeezed the loose clay grains of the till into a tight, natural concrete, which farmers call "hardpan." At Stonewall Beach, in between Wequobsque Cliffs and Squibnocket Point, the till seems to recede as if gathering further strength before approaching Squibnocket Cliffs. Then the chocolate-brown and gray till streaks across the bluffs and "coursing waters have carved strange cliff fantasies into it. Pointed spurs, steep gullies and eroded peaks provide all the appurtenances of a badlands," writes Barbara Blau Chamberlain in *These Fragile Outposts*.

In this foreground view, one can locate large boulders brought from the mainland by the glacier. These are dotted through the cliffs "like raisins in a pound cake" notes Chamberlain. Eventually undermined, they fall to the beach, spreading in unruly fashion like a carpet of cobblestones. This outwash formation contains mainland granite pieces, and ancient sharks' teeth have been found imbedded in its debris.

HERRING CREEK VIEW

From a vantage point near Herring Creek in Gay Head, this magnificent view over Menemsha Pond can be seen. On the clearest days the panorama also includes Vineyard Sound and the Elizabeth Island. Close by is another favorite viewpoint which overlooks Clam Point Cove. The latter spot is a favorite stop for tour busses as well as for photographers and artists whose cameras and paint brushes are poised to capture the scene.

In the far left is the site of Lobsterville, one of the Island's most important fishing villages a century ago. In those days boats arrived daily for captains to purchase fresh lobsters and fish for the big city markets. The little colony, which began around 1878 faded as Menemsha grew in importance.

On the south side of the highway (or back of the photographer) is Squibnocket Pond, largest body of fresh water on the Vineyard. Records indicate it was once open to the sea and tales are told of a whaling brig that anchored in the pond during a fog. Long before, this was a summering place of Indians.

It is the low, brush-covered land west of Squibnocket Pond that was recently, purchased by Jacqueline Kennedy Onassis. According to published reports, perservation was one of her objective in buying this tract of tranquil beauty where wild roses, bayberry, cranberries, dusty miller and coarse beach grass continue to provide cover for the four-legged and two-winged wild things.

Wealthy sportsmen came to Squibnocket Point for forty years or more, drawn by the availability of striped bass. Their New York Clubhouse was one of several bass clubs organized here after the Civil War. Several fishing shacks were on the point, along with the Humane Society Boathouse, a refuge for shipwrecked sailors.

74

GAY HEAD CLIFFS FROM THE AIR

The Wampanoags knew the west end of Martha's Vineyard as both Aquinnah, meaning "long end" or "point," and Kuhtuhquehtuut, meaning "on the great hill." Bartholomew Gosnold, when sighting the headlands in 1602, enthusiastically named them after England's Dover Cliffs. But today these National Landmarks are known the world over as the magnificent clay cliffs of Gay Head. Climbing on the cliffs and removal of fossils are forbidden.

William Baylies, one of the first geologists to see the mile-long sea cliffs, wrote that the first sight of them cured his seasickness. "Nothing could alleviate my feelings but a view of Gay head . . . at a distance of fifteen miles. A variety of colors such as red, yellow, and white, differently shaded and combined, exhibited a scene sufficient to captivate the mind, however distressed."

Gazing at them today, it is as if giant fingers had streaked dyes of red, green, tan, gray, yellow, dazzling white, and coal black across the face of the cliffs. Ancient fossils and glacials boulders protrude like knobby knuckles amid the layers which run horizontally, diagonally, and vertically in a pleasing jumble. This colorful confusion is, according to Chamberlain, like "the creased the shuffled pages of an ancient manuscript . . . New England's most complete record of its past hundred million years. It tells a story of land first covered with ancient forests, then engulfed by seawaters, laid bare and engulfed again; of giant sharks swimming over what are now the plains of Chilmark, of camels and horses roaming the plains where Gay Head now rises; of a series of overpowering invasions by ice floes from the north."

Standing guard over the cliffs is the Gay Head Light, at one time one of the most important on the Atlantic Coast. The first wooden lighthouse was built in 1799 after authorization by President John Adams. It housed one of the first revolving lights in the country. In 1859 a larger steel structure was erected and the unique Fresnel lens installed. This amazing light can be seen at the Dukes County Historical Society where it was retired from service once electricity and bull's-eye lenses came to Gay Head Light.

A JUMBLE OF COLOR AT GAY HEAD

Trickling waters carrying iron through the cliffs impart shades of red to the sand, gravel, and boulders. The darker rock is perodite, which is vaguely related to the rocks that produce diamonds elsewhere in the world. The blue shades come from a layer of stony blue clay and the dazzling white is gravel. All of these combine to produce a rusty, tarnished surface which gives an ancient, weathered look to the cliffs and to the gradually enlarging pile of boulders at their base. Gradually these cliffs are being eroded and the colorful debris stains the blue water as it sinks to the ocean floor.

The town of Gay Head has as colorful a history as that of the cliffs. From the beginning its inhabitants have been the Aquinnah group of the Martha's Vineyard Indians. When the English arrived, all lived under the Mayhew patent. In 1687 Governor Dongan of New York purchased the Indian rights from Sachem Joseph Mittark to be sure they were under his manorial grant. At this time the islands of Martha's Vineyard, the Elizabeth Chain, and Noman's Land were within the province of New York. When their citizens became part of the Massachusetts Bay Colony,they were known as the County of Dukes County. In 1711 the English Society for the Propagation of the Gospel in Foreign Parts purchased title to Gay Head. This was voided after the Revolution when this area became part of the Commonwealth of Massachusetts. Over the objections of the Indian people, Gay Head became incorporated into the Commonwealth of Massachusetts in 1870. It is, along with Mashpee on Cape Cod, one of the two Indian towns in the state. Through these various changes of government, life has continued much as usual.

Today there is increasing pride on the part of Indians and non-Indians in the ancient heritage. This was exemplified by Dr. Alvin Strock who recently gave to the tribe land containing the old cemetery at Gay Head.

GAY HEAD BAPTIST CHURCH, SYMBOL OF AQUINNAH HERITAGE

The congregation of this church officially began in 1693 and is considered to be the oldest Indian Baptist church in the country. (The Mashpee Baptist Church is older, having been organized in 1684, but did not become Baptist until after this one.) Its pastors have been mostly native sons. Silas Paul and Thomas Jeffers were two of the most noted, along with the original native missionary Sachem Joseph Mittark. He had brought Christianity to his people prior to his death in 1683, though formal organization was later. This, the congregation's third building, was dedicated in 1850 and stood originally on old South Road near the ancient graveyard.

The Gay Head (or Aquinnah) Indians were known the world over for their prowess as fishermen and whalers. The late Amos Smalley was noted as the only man to have harpooned a white whale. Joseph Belain spent sixty years as a whaler. It was considered good luck by captains to have a Gay Head Indian as a crew member.

Gay Head also has the distinction of being the annual rendezvous for the monarch butterflies as they prepare to migrate south. After rallying here by the thousands in early fall, they fly an astonishing pilgrimage each year to a 9,500-foot volcanic mountain in Mexico for the winter. The monarchs fly at a 15-foot altitude, going around buildings, through cities, and over coastal waters. They stop briefly to feed on flowers during the day and cluster at night in trees along the route. The publication of the National Wildlife Federation recently reported on this phenomena, noting that monarchs evolved in Mexico thousands of years ago. Gradually they have extended their breeding grounds northward, but each year they return to their ancient home.

MENEMSHA HARBOR'S FISHING SHACKS

When Menemsha Creek was dredged just after the turn of the century, and jetties were built to protect the entrance, the basin became a sheltering port for lobster and trap fishermen as well as for those who ventured farther out to sea. A tiny picturesque fishing village developed which today draws tourists, artists, and photographers in addition to fishermen.

When the Menemsha Bight (a bight according to Webster is a bend in the coast forming an open bay) is "matted with fish," anglers fish from the jetties and beaches while sports fishermen take to small boats to pull in bluefish, mackerel, bonito, and false albacore. Flocks of gulls and terns flying slowly over the shallows near Dogfish Bar herald the presence of large schools of fish. Occasionally the birds dart into the water and emerge triumphantly with lunch. Before World War II almost fifty commercial swordfish boats made Menemsha their headquarters, but today most of the boats are those of yachtsmen or pleasure fishermen.

One of the noted fishermen of Menemsha in earlier days was Captain Dan Flanders, eldest of three whaling brothers. He was a staunch Methodist and before sailing on whaling voyages would put into Menemsha Bight to get the parson's blessing. The Captain was a "Sunday whaler," which means that no whales were caught on Sundays during his voyages.

ROSES CASCADE OVER AN ANCIENT WALL

The sea air seems to encourage roses to bloom on the Vineyard throughout the warm months. An amazing variety of color and type can be seen, some in places where houses once stood. Though the houses and their inhabitants have long since disappeared, the roses continue to bloom faithfully each summer. The fragrance of these rose clusters scents the air and draws the velvety bumblebees.

This is the season for wildflowers too. Daisies and dandelions sprinkle the meadows. Pinky-lavender clover heads and yellow black-eyed Susans add color. Earlier arrivals are the frail, pink mayflowers, followed by lady's slippers. In patches across the meadows are the white blossoms of the beach plum. Fall is heralded by the goldenrod and the crimsons of the poison ivy and sumac. Indian pipes stand silently in wooded places, their stems like white wax with a touch of pink. Wild rose petals still cling tenaciously to their centers and field asters are pink and purple dots in the grass.

While discussing nature's offerings, we must not forget the birds. According to a recent *Vineyard Gazette,* spotters saw during one week an albino goldfinch, a black-throated blue warbler, three palm warblers, and many meadowlarks along with catbirds, field sparrows, Carolina wrens, and an indigo bunting. A beach watcher saw over 100 gannets, a horned grebe, and scaup ducks, while red-breasted mergensers were reported at Pocha Pond. This only records a few of the birds seen, but it's enough to show that Island remains a bird watcher's paradise.

ANCIENT STONE WALLS CRISSCROSS THE ISLAND

It has been said that most of the old stone walls on the Island were built by four men who made it a major business throughout their lifetimes. These men were assisted by oxen trained to move great stone weights and place their burdens with precision so the walls would be permanent. Whether or not this story is true, one thing is certain. Those early stone walls were permanent and still crisscross the land, particularly up-Island. These builders were proficient in "dry-dyking," the art of laying up the walls without cement.

Another ability developed by the early farmers was that of "ditching" or the art of reclaiming land by draining swamps. Afterwards, this process kept the low farmland from being overrun with rising water during heavy rains. By keeping the ditches free from leaves and twigs, the water ran constantly, keeping unhealthy stagnant areas at a minimum.

An additional reminder of early farming is West Tisbury's Agricultural Society's Hall. It was built in 1859 for the Society's annual fair, which continues each August. Folks from all over come to the tiny up-Island farming community to "oh" and "ah" over the crimson tomatoes, outsize pumpkins, and glowing jars of beach plum jelly on exhibit. Hopefuls compete for prizes with their luscious looking chocolate cakes, homemade clothing, and flower arrangements, as well as with their roosters, sheep, and sows. The draft horse pull always draws a crowd. Though there is a dustry midway which always seems more glamorous at night, the emphasis remains on the rural and agricultural tradition.

BOAT BUILDING IN THE BACKYARD

That the Vineyard remains a seafaring center is evidenced by this boat which is gradually taking shape in a backyard. This very typical activity began with the first settlers who needed boats to assist in fishing and to reach the mainland. Shipbuilding flourished in later years with the whaling era, and in the early part of this century the fishing fleet gained prominence. The many boats supported hundreds of families. Draggers were equally numerous, with the crew setting nets anywhere from ten to seventy-five miles out to sea. In recent years, due to a lessening supply of fish and the advent of huge European trawlers, this aspect of fishing has declined.

Yet, during one week in a recent fall, fishermen brought in a good supply of bay scallops and striped bass along with a few tuna. Cap'n Jimmie Morgan "who goes fishing wherever there is a damp spot anywhere," according to Joseph Chase Allen writing in the *Vineyard Gazette,* landed 500 pounds of dragged cod, a hundredweight of black-backed flounder, and two bluefish. Two offshore draggers came in with 17,000 cod and flounders and 7,000 pounds of scup. All told, says Allen, "up to Saturday, Vineyard Fish Co. had shipped 15 tons, split between New Bedford and New York. This was before the last off-shore vessel showed up."

Though the maritime history of the Vineyard includes several such periods of rising then waning, it seems clear that boats will always be a part of the Vineyard scene and this latest boat builder is not entirely a wide-eyed optimist.

THE TISBURY TOWN HALL AT VINEYARD HAVEN

The American flag and the carved seal near the roof line are clues that this white steepled building is a town hall rather than a church. Since 1920, the imposing structure had been the town hall of Tisbury (Vineyard Haven). In 1971, Katharine Cornell, the late actress who was one of the Island's famous residents, was instrumental in the restoration of the venerable building for the Tercentenary of the town. At that time the first floor offices were refurbished and the upstairs auditorium was completely redecorated. An artistic touch was added when the walls, and even the ceiling, were decorated with beautiful murals depicting Island scenes of both long ago and today. These historical paintings and current beach and ocean views give an elegant setting to meetings. Priscilla Patterson was commissioned to create the town seal which can be seen in this picture.

The building itself has a colorful history. It was erected in 1844 as a home for two congregations—Congregational and Baptist. The Congregationalists shared a minister with the parish at Edgartown. Then in 1884 this church became the meeting place of the Vineyard Literary Association. This group owned the building until Captain Gilbert Smith, a whale man, purchased it in 1890. It was he who sold this oldest ecclesiastical structure on the island to the town.

Currently these offices on Spring Street are busy places, for in this as well as in the other five town offices on the Island, residents and summer people obtain permits for taking shellfish, opening businesses, running tour buses, putting on shows, building a house or moving a driveway!

CYCLISTS ABOUT TO EXPLORE THE ISLAND

One of the nicest ways (and probably the healthiest) to explore Martha's Vineyard is with a bicycle. Not only are the roads fairly level and distances not too great, but there are many miles of bike paths. A separate paved path winds along the road from Oak Bluffs to Edgartown and there are many new ones in the State Forest. Since motorists are conditioned to expect cyclists, it is one of the easier places to ride. Many folks bring their own bicycles from the mainland, but there are plenty here and at other bike shops just waiting to be rented.

Diagonally across the street from the Bike Shop is the Seaman's Bethel. Purposely placed on the harbor, this missionary organization has served through the years as a "home away from home" for sailors. The first sailor's refuge, called the Sailor's Reading Room and Mission, was built in 1867 on the West Chop Shore. It was begun by Unitarian missionary Rev. David Waldo Stevens. Then in 1893 the present Seaman's Bethel was built and opened under the auspices of the Seamen's Friend Society in Boston. Chaplain Madison Edwards, who was assigned here from an earlier seamen's refuge at Tarpaulin Cove, Naushon Island, was missioner. At a time when hundreds of vessels were dropping anchor in the bustling harbor, the Bethel gave spiritual and social aid to sailors and outfitted those who had lost everything by shipwreck. Sailors could browse in the library, write letters home, visit with their friends, and join in the occasional hymn sings.

Presently the little haven consists of a museum and simple chapel. Historical exhibits of all types, including the work of whale men on their ships, absorb the visitor. A few moments spent in the quiet chapel with its brilliant stained-glass sea-motif window revives the spirits.

92

WEST CHOP'S TRAVELING LIGHTHOUSE

Guarding the western end of Vineyard Haven Harbor is West Chop Lighthouse which has been moved back from eroding banks several times. Erected in 1817, it was increased to its present height in 1891. It now stands 84 feet above sea level. The last lighthouse to be manned on the Island, it sends a comforting beam on starry nights and during foggy hours moans a rhythmic warning signal across Vineyard Sound.

The lighthouse presides over a community that had several beginnings. In the 1870's at "The Neck" both Cedar Bluff and West Point Grove developments began, but these resulted in only a few streets and a wharf. Then in 1887 a group of Boston businessmen formed the West Chop Light Company, purchasing sizable land from whaling merchant Captain William Lewis. Soon a summer colony developed as the resort era began. A steamboat made regular calls and a brisk maritime business began, which later gave way to the growing maritime establishments at Vineyard Haven Harbor.

Occasionally there is speculation on how "The Chops" were named. Some think it was because these two headlands resemble two cuts of meat. Others believe it was because they resemble the jaws (or chops) of a vise. Actually it is an Old English term that describes a harbor or channel entrance.

94